I AM

Joe Evans
Cassie Waits

I AM
ISBN: Softcover 978-1-955581-26-4
Copyright © 2021 by Joe Evans and Cassie Waits

All rights reserved. No part of this book may be reproduced or transmitted in any form or by any means, electronic or mechanical, including photocopying, recording, or by any information storage and retrieval system, without permission in writing from the publisher.

Parson's Porch Books is an imprint of Parson's Porch *& Company* (PP*&*C) in Cleveland, Tennessee. PP*&*C is an innovative organization which raises money by publishing books of noted authors, representing all genres. Its face and voice is **David Russell Tullock** (dtullock@parsonsporch.com).

Parson's Porch *& Company turns books into bread & milk* by sharing its profits with the poor.

www.parsonsporch.com

I AM

*This book is dedicated to Mary Ella Nunn
in remembrance of her many years of ministry
in Christian Education at
First Presbyterian Church of Marietta.*

Contents

With Gratitude 6
Preface 8
I AM the Bread of Life 11
   Deuteronomy 8: 1-9 and John 6: 35, 41-51 11
I AM The Light of the World 21
   John 8: 12-20 and Isaiah 58: 1-9 21
I AM the Gate 32
   Proverbs 8: 1-11 and John 10: 1-10 32
I AM the Good Shepherd 42
   John 10: 11-18 and Psalm 23 42
I AM The Resurrection and the Life 53
   John 11: 17-27 and Ezekiel 37: 1-14 53
I AM the Way and the Truth and the Life 65
   Exodus 13: 17-22 and John 14: 1-7 65
I AM the Vine 76
   Isaiah 5: 1-7 and John 15: 1-8 76
I AM 86
   Exodus 3: 1-14 and John 18: 1-11 86
Final Thoughts 97

With Gratitude

This book was made possible by:

Bob Brown, who loved this series and encouraged us to publish it

Sue Strauss and George Evans, who took pictures of the authors

Kelly Dewar, who created the cover and promoted the sermon series

Becca Yan, who edited, clarified, and, just generally, made this book better

Tim Hammond and Howard Swinford, who created the chicken wire structure which provided the congregation a place to hang their prayers

Buni Ricketts, who provided so many of the ribbons and whose legacy lives on

And the countless others who inspired us

Preface

"It was the best of times, it was the worst of times, it was the age of wisdom, it was the age of foolishness, it was the epoch of belief, it was the epoch of incredulity…"
A Tale of Two Cities, Charles Dickens

The Summer of 2021 was a strange time, to say the least. Some were rushing to be vaccinated; others were determined not to be. While there was plenty of hope, joy, and excitement, I remember it as a time of division, anxiety, fear, illness, and death as cases of COVID-19 were rising again. Many resolved to live as though everything were back to normal.

How would I shepherd this congregation through this once-in-a-century crisis? The pandemic upended our faith practices, transformed our approach to sacraments, and fundamentally altered what it meant to be "gathered" in God's presence. Everything had changed, and yet, our God had not changed.

The Rev. Cassie Waits wondered if we might encourage the congregation to find hope in this tumultuous time. She proposed an eight-week sermon series on the "I AM" statements of Jesus. Eight times in the gospel of John, Jesus describes himself by saying, "I am…" This was good enough for me, but Cassie had more. She wanted us to "do something."

I'm not really one for creative ideas in worship. I even wear the same shoes every Sunday. Switching out the laces every once in a while is variety enough for me! I trust Cassie, though, so we kicked her idea around with a few other wise church staff people (Mary Groves, especially), and a plan was born. Each Sunday would have a different-colored ribbon. On those ribbons, the congregation would write a response to the sermon: a prayer, a word, a challenge. Throughout the summer, the ribbons would be tied to a structure outside, built by Tim Hammond and Howard Swinford. The wind would blow through those ribbons, lifting our prayers to Almighty God.

It was the most important sermon series I've ever been a part of.

The sermons in this book are the sermons that we preached. Each sermon ends with a prayer and nudge to you to "do something" with them. You might find your own ribbons to write on, or you might write a letter to the person whom the sermon made you remember. Whatever you do, do something so that you be not "hearers of the word only, but doers" (James 1: 22).

Joe Evans
Marietta, GA

I AM the Bread of Life
Deuteronomy 8: 1-9 and John 6: 35, 41-51

Preached on June 6, 2021 by Rev. Joe Evans

Today begins a sermon series that will last the summer based on what Bible scholars call the "I Am" statements. On several different occasions, Jesus tells those who are listening who he is using statements like the one we just read: "I AM the bread of life." On this communion Sunday, we recognize that this statement is both a metaphor and a fact. When he says, "I AM the bread of life," we know that he's not just like bread. He is the bread.

Even more than the mother bird who made a nest outside our kitchen window and flies back and forth all day feeding her two chicks, we don't just thank the one who "gives us this day our daily bread" today. We gather around the table remembering the one who loves us so much that he offers us his body and his blood.

I AM the bread of life.

That's love in a most profound sense, and we know he loves us by this gift that he provides. Not everyone loves us that much.

"I AM the bread of life," he says, and as he says it, we know he loves us even more than the waitress at Red Lobster who brings those delicious biscuits to the table ruining our appetite. Do you know the biscuits I'm talking about? In the ancient world, in the culture of ancient Israel and Palestine, bread wasn't like that. It wasn't a treat. It wasn't something that you had on special occasions. Back then, when people thought of bread, they weren't thinking about carbs; they were thinking about the most basic form of sustenance, the most basic staple at the dinner table. When Jesus says bread, he's talking about the grain of life.

It's what rice is to so much of Asia.

What grits were to our Southern fore parents.

Not what french fries or chicken nuggets are to our kids and grandkids.

Bread isn't junk food in the sense that Jesus means it, though sometimes we think that the ones who provide us with junk food must love us the most. That's why, when I make the girls desert, I give them as big an ice cream scoop as I can. I do that because I want to be their favorite, but there is another parent who loves them so much that she wants to make sure their teeth don't rot out.

"I AM the bread of life."

Bread is solid. It's nourishing.

It's not what you want but what you need.

The ones who love us the most supply us with bread.

I think about Jesus saying, "I AM the bread of life," and I remember this story that author Ann Lamott tells. She said that she was at a women's Bible study and the leader invited the women at the table to think of someone who was like Jesus to them. "Who embodied the Gospel to you? Who revealed to you God's love?" the leader asked. The ladies went around the table. You can imagine what they said.

One woman talked about how when she was growing up her grandmother lived right next door. When she'd had a bad day at school, she'd first stop at her grandmother's house on her way home, and somehow her grandmother seemed to know that she would be coming. Just as she walked in the door, Grandma would be pulling chocolate chip cookies out of the oven. "She was like Jesus to me," she said, and you can imagine what she meant.

Another told about her old golden retriever who was always there, bringing comfort, all through her divorce. Another talked about her sister. Another her father. On and on, amazing tales of kindness were told until the last woman at the table spoke: "Who has been like Jesus to me? That's a hard question to answer because Jesus loved people so much that he always told them the truth even if they didn't want to hear it. To answer this question, I have to think of someone who loved me so much that he was so honest with me that I wanted to kill him."

That's bread.

That's a particular kind of nourishment.

Certainly, we all need the warmth of a grandmother's chocolate chip cookies or the comforting presence of a good dog, but there is a powerful love in honesty. There's a love in bread that's more than the love in junk food.

Have you ever thought about how much junk food there is in the world?

How many people, how many of us, only read the journalists we already agree with?

How many of us think we're watching the news, only it's not really the news because it's not really the truth?

I tell you, if you can watch it without it making you uncomfortable, it's not bread. It's junk food because it doesn't nourish us though it tastes good. It's not bread, and it's certainly not love because the people who have really loved us sit us down to tell us those uncomfortable truths, like:

"You're just wrong, and I don't love you any less, but you've been wrong for a long time."

"I hate to say it, but you really have been drinking too much, and I'm worried about you."

"I don't want to be the one to tell you this, but you're showing up late and leaving early, and I love you and this organization too much not to bring it to your attention."

Of course, it's easier for me to be told that I'm doing a great job all the time and that I'm perfectly wonderful; however, that's not enough, and it's not the truth. I have two kinds of friends: one kind who will take my side no matter what and are glad to tell me that my wife Sara is always wrong, and my boss never appreciated me, and surely the ones who are criticizing me are idiots. Then I have another kind of friend who I call when I'm ready to hear the truth. This is the kind of friend we have in Jesus. He is the bread of life. He is not the fast food, fill you up then leave you empty, tastes good but clogs your arteries kind of savior.

"I AM the bread of life," he told them.

That's different, and people don't always like it.

The religious authorities of the day certainly didn't like it.

Our second Scripture lesson just calls them the Jews. That's not an exact title because not all the Jews were giving Jesus a hard time; some of the Jews were following him, and one of the Jews was him. What we know about the Gospel of John was that it was written so long after Jesus' death that the author had distanced himself from the Jewish community and wasn't familiar enough with all the major players to call them by name. I say that just so you know that some people within every community don't like the truth tellers.

People haven't changed very much over the last 2,000 years, so even today some people try to silence the truth tellers. They'd rather be fed fast food all the time. I guess we all would, though a diet of fast food doesn't give us the energy we need to change, and like the Hebrew people, wandering around the desert and not sure how to get to the Promised Land, for months now we've been living in a pandemic. There's a way out it seems, and I'll tell you how to find out which of the voices in our world are telling us the truth: it's the ones who don't tell us what we want to hear, but what we need to hear.

Who loves us enough to tell us to take our medicine?

Who is like the bread of life?

When you walked into the worship service this morning, with your bulletin came a brown ribbon. This is my first time buying a whole bunch of ribbons. It's hard to find enough brown for this many people. I tried to convince some church staff members that the colors I was able to find easily, tan and burnt orange, were close enough to brown. They didn't buy it. Then I tried to just cut them straight across. If you got one with ugly edges, I cut it; if you got one with a nice, diagonal cut, Natalie Foster probably did it. What I want you to do with those ribbons is think for just a minute about someone who has been like bread to you.

It could be a doctor who told you a hard truth and helped you to make some changes.

A teacher who wouldn't put up with your excuses.

A friend who dared to hold up a mirror to you and held your hand as she did it.

It might not have been what you wanted, but it sure was what you needed, to paraphrase the Rolling Stones. Think about a person who has been a gift from God to you, not because they were just kind, but because they helped you become a better you. Think about someone who has been like Jesus, the bread of life, and use a pen in the pocket of the chair right in front of you to write their name on your ribbon.

As for me, I'll be writing my wife Sara's name because she always loves me enough to tell me the truth, but I'm also writing George on my ribbon today. Back at Good Shepherd Presbyterian Church, the first church I served as a pastor, a mother once asked me to baptize her baby. I told her I would, but then the Senior Pastor told me she wanted to do the baptism. I said that would be fine, only no one ever told the mother which pastor would be doing the baptism. Right up at the front of the church, this mother tried to hand me her baby. The Senior Pastor took the baby instead. She baptized him in front of the whole church, while his mother stared me down like I'd just broken her heart.

I told George all this the next day over breakfast.

He was a young pastor then too, and I said, "Can you believe that Senior Pastor? Can you believe she wouldn't just let me do the baptism? And why didn't she call the mother?"

George wasn't hearing any of that.

He just looked me in the eye, and he said, "Joe, you messed up. And I mean, you really messed up. But it's going to be OK because I know you'll make it right and you won't make this same mistake again."

In that moment, George was like Jesus to me because he told me the truth that I needed to hear. He spoke the words that helped me do better and be better. His words helped me to become a better man and a better pastor, so today I'll be writing George's name on my ribbon, giving thanks to God for him.

At the end of the service, we'll all go outside and tie our ribbons on a structure that has chicken wire that Tim Hammond and Howard Swinford built for us. As the wind blows through our ribbons in the coming weeks, the wind will lift our prayers of gratitude to God for those who have been like bread to us and our prayers of gratitude for nurturing us with the true bread from heaven and food of eternal life.

Take just a moment now, as a prayer of thanksgiving, to write down the name of someone who has been like bread to you.

Amen.

Practice: Who has been like bread to you? How can you thank them?

Prayer: *Jesus Christ, bread of life, thank you for all the ways that you nourish me. Grant me the courage to hear the truth and* to be changed by it. In our world of fluff and empty words, help me to hear the truth, especially the truth that your love for me never changes. Amen.

I AM The Light of the World
John 8: 12-20 and Isaiah 58: 1-9

Preached on June 13, 2021 by Rev. Cassie Waits

Dr. Bob Harper warned me. He warned me to wear sunscreen at the beach. Dr. Harper is a dermatologist, and he knows these things.

Three hours into the beach, I'm deep into Matthew McConaughey's new book, *Greenlights*. I can see why it's a New York Times bestseller. I'm so engrossed that I don't notice my back is getting more than just a light tan.

"You're turning pink!" Mom exclaims. Turns out, sunscreen only works when you apply it.

We need sunscreen because the sun is powerful. It blisters our skin and damages our eyes, but we can't avoid sunlight either. Sunlight gives us Vitamin D. It regulates our sleep cycles. It even regulates our mood.

The sun has power.

Human beings have recognized and revered this power for millennia. Sun worship doesn't begin on the beaches of Florida, after all.

The ancient Egyptians worshipped the sun. Their sun god was called Re ("ray") – that's a pretty good name for a sun god. Re is the Creator and Nourisher of the earth. Re is the *light of their world*.

Ancient India had Surya – the all-seeing sun god, who banished darkness and evil and disease. Surya is the *light of their world*.

First century Romans worshipped the sun god Mithra: protector of the truth, possessor of the all-seeing eye. Sailors trusted Mithra to keep them safe during storms. Soldiers trusted Mithra to protect them in battle. Ordinary folks trusted Mithra to provide for their needs.

Mithra was not just a footnote in the vast Roman pantheon. In a dark and tumultuous first century, Mithra promised hope. Mithra inspired followers to form communities of faith. For those followers, Mithra was the *light of the world*.

Then Jesus comes along, offering a counter-message:

"I am the light of the world.

Whoever follows ME will never walk in darkness."

These words kick off a debate with some Pharisees.

Jesus says: "I am the light of the world."

They respond: "Oh yeah? Says who?"

We usually demonize the Pharisees, but I appreciate their question. Are you really the light of the world, Jesus?

We would do well to ask this question ourselves when someone or something promises to be the light of our world. It's all too easy to believe a lie, get turned around, and follow the wrong light.

It's easy to get lost.

The rite of passage at my middle school was the seventh-grade trip to Washington, D.C. For one week, we got to enjoy a charter bus with a bathroom. This was a step up from the regular school bus, and we went around, site to site, for a hands-on experience of U.S. government and history.

Before we got on the bus, we got a partner. We were to sit with our partner and keep up with our partner.

I sat with my best friend, Becky. Across the aisle were our friends Scott and Brandon. We did that so we could talk during the 12-hour trip.

The first afternoon, we got off the bus to see the Lincoln Memorial. Then we all got back on the bus to go to dinner. All of us, except for Brandon.

Only we didn't realize it. We were halfway to dinner before *anyone* realized that Brandon wasn't there.

Personally, I blame Scott. Scott was Brandon's partner. Scott should have spoken up. And I blame Becky! This was not the first time Brandon had gotten lost on a class field trip. He had a history, and she knew it. Why didn't she say something?

But I also blame myself. What kind of friend doesn't notice that you're not even on the bus?

Brandon would go on to earn a Ph.D. in Physics. Today, he does research for a company whose products you have in your home. He's one of the smartest people I have ever known, but on that day, he was 700 miles from home, in an unfamiliar city, stumbling around in the dark. He lost the tour guide, the teachers, the whole class.

And he started following the wrong person.

We've all done it.

We've all followed the wrong thing. We've all hitched our hopes to the wrong wagon.

Now, we don't have Mithra these days, or Re, or Surya, but we have plenty of other things vying to be the light of our world.

What's the light of your world?

Where do you hang your hope?

Are you relying on your reputation? Or your family? Or your social group to give you meaning and purpose?

Is your hope is tied to future success? Or the success of your kids? In being accepted or promoted or rewarded?

Are you hoping in your nest egg? Or your paycheck? Or in the enjoyment of possessions?

Maybe you've rejected all this and decided that the only one you can trust is yourself. Are you hanging your hope on your own hard work and talent and determination?

What is it that you are pursuing at all costs? Because that thing – *that thing* – is the light of your world.

There are many places we might put our hope in instead of Jesus.

The gospel of John talks a lot about light, and John uses 'the light' as a metaphor for Jesus. What does 'the light' do?

1. The light REVEALS truth.
2. The light EXPOSES sin.
3. The light brings HEALING.
4. The light brings HOPE.

In Matthew's gospel, during the Sermon on the Mount, Jesus turns things around.

He tells his followers: "You are the light of the world…a city on a hill cannot be hidden…a lamp on its stand gives light to the whole house. [so] Let your light shine before others."

Friends, we are not to stand by and marvel at the light of Jesus. We are to carry it ourselves. We are tasked with revealing truth, exposing sin, healing wounds, and sharing the hope we have with a lost and broken world.

Living into this calling takes courage. It takes courage to notice when someone is lost and hurting. It takes courage to intervene.

One Christmas, my husband and I ran into Tim. We hadn't seen Tim in months. No one had seen Tim in months. He said he'd been "busy." That day, he looked a little disheveled. His skin was a little too yellow, and his words were a little too confused.

I'd like to tell you that I noticed the signs of alcoholism, that I intervened and insisted he get help. I didn't.

Other more courageous friends did. They showed up on his doorstep. They escorted him to the hospital. They learned the horrifying truth: he needed a lot of help and a new liver.

The light reveals what we don't want to see. The light forces us to take action. When we carry the light, we open the door to healing and new life.

Carrying the light is hard work. Carrying the light is holy work.

This church knows how to carry the light. When Adrean and Clyde Grant had their baby, Sue Velardi showed up on the doorstep with dinner to celebrate and offer support and encouragement during those stressful early days.

Wanda Reese was having trouble joining a Zoom Bible study. Melodie Clayton tried to help her over the phone, and when that didn't work, Melodie got in her car and drove to Wanda's house. They figured it out, but even if they hadn't, Melodie made sure that Wanda would not struggle alone.

We've been praying for Carolyn Tiede for a while. She was diagnosed unexpectedly with advanced cancer. This was devastating. She was still digesting the news when she ran into Ray Fountain at the oncologist's office, and in that moment of fear and uncertainty, Ray encouraged her. I can't imagine a better person to meet at the oncologist. Ray gave her his phone number and told her to call anytime.

Yes, this church knows how to carry the light.

We also carry the light of Christ in our worship service. Every week, we light these two candles on the communion table. (You might have thought these candles were just nice decorations!) These candles are physical reminders that we are in the presence of the light of the world.

We carry the flame into the Sanctuary for worship, and then we carry it out as we go forth to share that light with others.

The thing about these candles is that they require maintenance. During the pandemic, your worship leaders learned a lot of new tricks, but we never did get the hang of maintaining the candles.

Every service, they would flame up like blowtorches and then slowly die out. By the time we got to the sermon, there would be nothing left but smoke. They need a certain amount of oil, a certain length of wick.

These candles need care if they are to carry the light. We, too, need maintenance to carry the light. That's why faith is a *discipline*. You don't say a prayer and move on. You have to replenish the oil and trim the wick.

If you are going to carry the light, you have to stay in relationship with the light.

So we worship.

We pray.

We study scripture.

We do life with other Christians.

We encourage and care for one another.

We serve the vulnerable.

This is how we stay in the light, and when we are in the light, we find the courage to love one another so much that we will wade into the discomfort and the mess and the brokenness with them.

Tim's friends waded into the brokenness. They refused to be brushed off, and they saved his life that day. That was a miracle.

Still, they couldn't save Tim in the end.

See, we may point to the savior, but only Jesus can save. We cannot save even ourselves.

Standing at Tim's graveside, the pastor reassured us that death does not have the final say. Our hope is not in the things of this world – our hope is in the light of the world.

In this world, we will face difficulty and grief, and yet, we will sing in the midst of tragedy, press on in the face of fear, and claim victory at the grave. We will take heart because the true light of the world is shining, and the darkness has not, will not, and cannot overcome it.

Amen.

Practice: Where is your light coming from today? What is vying for the place of Jesus in your life? Sum it up in a word and write it down on a ribbon or a piece of paper. Then release it, and let it go, that the true light of the world might take its place.

Prayer: Lord Jesus, forgive us for following the wrong things. Fill our hearts with your true light, that we might put our hope in you alone. Amen.

I AM the Gate
Proverbs 8: 1-11 and John 10: 1-10

Preached on June 20, 2021 by Rev. Joe Evans

About four years ago, we moved here from Columbia, Tennessee. As we moved into our new house, the first order of business was building a fence in the backyard for our two dogs, Lucy and Junebug. I worked on this project with a couple new Marietta friends, Clem Doyle and Paul Phillips, who volunteered to help me.

You can tell now just by looking at the fence which parts Paul was involved in.

I remember Clem and I eyeballing the fence slats while Paul got a string and a level going to make sure things lined up precisely. You might say engineers (Paul) are better at these kinds of things than attorneys (Clem) or preachers (me). To this day, four years later, it's still a very good-looking fence, and I can't put into words how much it meant to me that Paul and Clem would come over to help me build it. However, they couldn't help me with everything. Even with their help, there were a couple things I had to do on my own since it was our fence. For example, no one else could choose where the gates would go.

"I AM the gate," Jesus said.

If you have a fence in your backyard, think about it for just a moment.

Where did you put your gates, and what does your gate mean to you?

What are the gates there for?

Who goes through them and why?

In our backyard, one gate opens into the yard of the next-door neighbor. The day we moved in, we were greeted by them. Their names are Dan and Leanne. I remember how un-neighborly it felt to immediately build a fence between us so soon after meeting them. We didn't mean to fence them out, we just wanted to fence our dogs in, so I put a gate there from our yard to theirs. We built the fence and the gate and, on their side, now stones are lined up to make a path. They built up a flower bed on either side of the path that leads to our gate in their yard. We built the gate, and they built a path. Today, it's like an invitation to go from one yard to the other.

"I AM the gate," Jesus said.

What we know is that he is like an open invitation from God to be in relationship.

What's required to go through?

Who is fenced out?

He makes the way clear and invites us all to come in.

Jesus spends all this time trying to convince us that a relationship with God is not nearly so complicated as we had imagined, and I wonder if we imagine a relationship with God much be complicated because relationships with people are.

We're always asking: who should I let in?

How much should I let them in?

Will they disappoint me?

Will they take advantage of me?

Do they like me?

Relationships require a lot, so I think it's good to be in charge of the gates around our yards. It's not good for a family not to have any boundaries or limits. If we didn't have a fence, our dogs would be eating out of every neighbor's garbage can, and our children might be, too. It's important to have a fence.

Rev. Joe Brice will remind us from time to time that we humans need boundaries the same way that cells need a cell wall. Without a cell wall, the cell has no identity. The same is true of us. Without some limits, we become blobs of availability, victims to the circumstances around us, so we must have limits, boundaries, and fences.

Right across the street from our house, there was a house with a swimming pool in the back. The family put up a flagpole to send out a signal to the neighborhood: when the flag was up that meant any who wanted could come over and swim, but when the flag was down, that meant that the gate was closed. The family needed time to swim, just them. That makes sense, and we must all decide on the gates of our own homes while recognizing who is the gate into the Kingdom of Heaven.

There's an old story that goes like this: a Presbyterian died. He was welcomed into heaven by St. Peter through the Pearly Gates, and right away, he met an Episcopalian he went to college with. The Presbyterian was really excited to see his old friend, but the Episcopalian told him to keep his voice down. "Why do I need to be so quiet in heaven?" he asked. The Episcopalian answered: "It's because the Baptists are right over that hill. They think they're the only ones who made it up here, and we don't want to spoil it for them."

You can make that joke about Baptists or whomever you want. It's true in one sense for all of us. We all get tied up in debates over who is in and who is out as though the Kingdom of Heaven were a bigger version of our own backyards. It's not. "I AM the gate," he said, and we could all stand to learn a thing or two from him when it comes to the gates around our own homes and lives, for leaving people out can hurt them.

Have you ever been left outside of the gate?

Years ago, this church supported me as a missionary intern to Argentina. There I lived with several Argentinean college students who were nice enough to befriend me and help me make my way around the city of La Plata. One Saturday night, they thought it would be fun to take me to a dance club. It was the only time I've stood outside of a club hoping the bouncer would let me in. My friends encouraged me to speak English very loudly so that the bouncer would notice that I was American. Being American will get us in a lot of places, but not this particular club in Argentina, apparently, because we never made it inside.

Have you ever been fenced out?

"I AM the gate," Jesus said.

In one parable, he spoke of great banquets hosted by a bridegroom who invited wealthy, upright, wellborn guests to a party. They chose not to show up, so the bridegroom went to the streets and invited society's castaways: the poor, the homeless, the rejected, the ones who are left out and left behind. The ones we are slow to invite in ourselves. "I AM the gate," he said, and we must consider what kind of a gate this savior is. We all need to think about whom he invites in and who has been kind enough to invite us in.

"I AM the gate," he said, and I'm prone to believe that what he means here is something like what author and journalist Kelly Corrigan meant in her graduation speech at the Walker School just a couple weeks ago. She told the graduates to remember that more than wealth, influence, or career accomplishments, the true source of human happiness comes from meaningful relationships.

"I AM the gate," Jesus said.

In that simple statement, he reminds us that there is something sacred about walking into our neighbor's yard; there is something miraculous that happens to children when they know they are safe to run from one house to another. Something special happens when we fire up the charcoal grill. The smoke doesn't respect our fences. Our neighbors wonder what we're cooking, and it makes us happier to share of our abundance than to eat it all ourselves.

Years ago, I cut grass for a living, and I cut grass for a company who never wanted to pay us overtime, so on Fridays, we'd often get sent home early, having already worked our 40 hours. That meant that sometimes the men I worked with would invite me over to their apartment for lunch. These guys were from Mexico. The six or seven, they all lived in a one-bedroom apartment to save money so that there would be more to send back home to their families. After going to the liquor store to cash their checks, we'd have lunch, most often tacos, cooked by whoever happened to be in charge of the meal that day. Only once did I invite the group over to our place, also a one-room apartment that just Sara and I shared. I cooked something and offered them a beer I had made myself. I was into homebrewing beer back then, and I thought that was a special thing to share; only one of the guys said to me that the special thing about it was that this was his first time being inside a white person's home.

"I AM the gate," Jesus said.

What he means by this is not exactly clear, but I believe it is clear enough to point us towards thinking about large and small ways that our lives might change if we spent more time thinking about whom we let into our homes and our lives. I think that's important because when I think for just a minute about those moments where I felt the genuine hospitality of a stranger, the genuine hospitality of a stranger who would become a friend, I could feel that something sacred was happening because genuine hospitality is nothing short of a miraculous thing.

"I AM the gate," he said.

Too often we go looking for God on pilgrimages to the Promised Land.

Too often we think that finding God demands climbing up a mountain or fasting and praying for days on end. Let me remind you, though, that Jesus said, "when two or more are gathered, God is present," so if you want to glimpse Jesus this week, just think about the places in your life where there is a fence now but there could be a gate.

Once again, you have a ribbon.

This is the third Sunday in a row when your pastors are asking you to do a little something different. Each Sunday this summer, we'll be asking you to write something on a different-colored ribbon and to tie those ribbons on the chicken-wire structure just outside the church. Today, your ribbon is gray or silver, to help all of us think about the gate. Today, I'd love for you to write the name of a person who you pray would let you in.

On this Father's Day, I've been thinking about John. John is not my father. My father's name is George, but were it not for my father, there would be a fence between John and me. Instead, there is a gate.

What happened is that John and I were playing baseball in Laurel Park when we were 8 or 9. He was playing catcher without a facemask. I was batting without knowing how to lay my bat down after I hit the ball. The pitcher pitched, I swung and hit, then slung the bat right at John's front teeth. I couldn't get out an apology. I just remember all John's blood on the grass and all my shame in my belly, for I was sure that I had ruined everything and should never have been born. Dad was not so sure about any of that. In fact, Dad was sure John would not hate me forever, we didn't need to move away, and I could play baseball again. Dad was sure there could still be a gate, and with those simple words that he pushed me to say, "I'm sorry," miraculously there was one.

Where do you long for a gate?

With whom?

Write his/her name down on your ribbon, and as the wind blows through our ribbons, our prayers will be lifted to the one who by his grace is "the gate."

Amen.

Practice: Where is there a wall between you and someone you love? Who is leaving you out? Who are you leaving out? Where in your life do you long for a gate? Write the name of a person whom you long to have a renewed relationship with down on a ribbon or a piece of paper. Release that relationship to God, and may Almighty God bless your life with a gate.

Prayer: *Almighty God, it is hard to be left out. I miss _____, and I long for a renewed relationship with him/her. Soften his/her heart to me. Soften my heart to him/her. Create a gate where now there is a wall, and may this change start with me. Amen.*

I AM the Good Shepherd
John 10: 11-18 and Psalm 23

Preached on June 27, 2021 by Rev. Joe Evans

Please read this second Scripture lesson, Psalm 23, with me.

Thank you for being willing to go out on a limb with me. I know that many of you have that memorized. Others, like me, need to cheat by reading it.

Memorizing has always been a little difficult for me.

It's one of those things that makes me so nervous that my brain sort of short-circuits.

I remember vividly an assignment to memorize and recite the Emancipation Proclamation in 9th grade history class. At some point during my recitation, I drifted into the Pledge of Allegiance. Has anything like that ever happened to you?

A lot of us have a sad public-speaking story.

I heard a statistic that there are more people whose number one fear is public speaking than anything else.

That means that there are more people whose number one fear is public speaking than there are people whose number one fear is death. Quoting this statistic, comedian Jerry Seinfeld said, "That means most people at a funeral would rather be the one in the casket than the one giving the eulogy." I don't know how exactly to make sense of that, but I believe it because what's true is that fears don't have to make complete sense to hold us captive.

We can be afraid of things that aren't even real because fear isn't entirely rational.

The question I pose to you this morning is, what do you do about it?

What or who brings you comfort?

Years ago, before we had kids, we had a dog named Ramona that we treated like a kid. Ramona was scared to death of thunder. During one thunderstorm, we couldn't find her and thought maybe she had run away. Searching the house, we finally found her nestled with some dirty clothes in the front-loading washing machine.

Have you ever heard of a dog doing that?

It sounds crazy, but then you think how much safer the washing machine is during a storm than the couch.

Now, our dogs just snuggle up real close to us on the couch when they're afraid, and probably, if a tree fell on the house or something like that, they'd be better off in a washing machine. More than that, though, if there's a scary storm moving over our house, the whole household might end up on the basement couch: two dogs, two girls, two adults, all together.

I don't know what they think Sara or I could do for them during a thunderstorm; still, they're there with us because they're scared and being close to us makes them feel better.

That might be true in your house, too.

Do you have dogs or cats or kids who huddle up next to you when they're scared?

And is that true of you as well?

Is there someone whose lap you remember crawling up into?

Or is there a person who, with just the smell of his aftershave, makes you feel safe?

Is there a house that makes you breathe a sigh of relief once you walk through its doors?

Does the smell of mothballs or ivory soap remind you of a person who made you feel comfortable enough to really talk about what was bothering you?

"I AM the good shepherd," he said, and his presence makes his sheep feel safe.

This is the fourth Sunday in a row of a sermon series focused on the ways Jesus describes himself, and what I'll always remember about this "I AM" statement, the fourth of eight that we're focusing on this summer, is that Pope Francis once said, "A shepherd must always smell like his sheep."

What he means by this is that Jesus is close enough to smell like us.

When we're scared, he's near, unlike the hired hand who runs away to save himself when trouble looms. It's because of this proximity, his familiarity, that he can cast out our fear. That's a wonderful truth, which matters today because today, there's a lot to be afraid of. What, though, do we do about it?

These days it's like the whole world is swallowed up in fear.

Just think about how often you've been seeing words like stress and anxiety. Those are two palatable words that adults are willing to use to talk about their fear.

Grownups aren't supposed to be afraid. No one likes to admit that he's scared, so we use words like stress and anxiety, even though anxiety is just fear, essentially. However, it's worse than fear because anxiety is a feeling that fills your body without a clear source. Anxiety is fear without knowing what you're afraid of.

It's always better to put a word to it or a cause.

Parents know that, and so they'll always ask their kids, "What are you so scared of?"

On the other hand, sometimes the girls will notice that I'm tense and kind of quiet. They'll ask me what's wrong, so I'll tell them I'm just a little stressed. It seems like I used to be stressed about certain things: sermons, projects, staffing, annual reviews. Lately, some days I'm just stressed, and I can't seem to put into words what it is that I'm stressed about. I just am. Can you relate?

It's a little bit crazy to be afraid without being able to say what we're afraid of, although you can imagine how we got this way.

When we were kids, maybe we'd wake up from a nightmare and would call for one of our parents. If we were lucky, one of them would rush in. Mom or Dad would ask, "Honey, what's the matter?"

"I had a nightmare," we'd respond.

"What was it about?" one of our parents would ask.

This is kind of an embarrassing question to answer.

Are you just supposed to come out and say, "I was in my classroom but only had on my underwear"? Can you just say out loud, as a grown-up, "I was being followed by a legion of life-sized caterpillars who were trying to eat me"? I guess it depends. How well do you know the person who asked?

Can you trust him with your fears?

Can you speak it out loud in her presence?

I hope you have someone you can talk to about the deepest concerns of your heart.

Life gives us heavy things to carry around, while so many people won't let anyone share the burden. Why? It's because we don't always trust the smell of the people who are asking.

There's a virus out there, sort of.

Who can you talk to about it? I don't know.

That's a scary thing to just start talking about because if you drive into the city, they're scared of you if you don't have a mask on. If you drive north of here, they think you're crazy if you're still wearing one. Some are watching the spread of the Delta variant while others are obsessed with getting a good deal on a Delta flight. Jobs are changing, the economy is changing, people are moving, so much is up in the air, and it's hard to know exactly what the future holds. More than that, it's hard to know whom you can trust to talk to about your worries for the future.

"I AM the good shepherd."

What does he mean by that?

He means, "I'm with you."

If you're scared, come on and climb up on the sofa with me, and tell me what you're so afraid of. I won't laugh. I'll just listen. I won't judge. I'll just be here. You can tell me. "I AM the good shepherd," he said, and he can cast out our fear so that we can get on moving towards where we are destined to go.

Yesterday, I read about a child of our church who hit a big milestone. James Whittingham is a baseball player, and early this season he made a goal for himself: 100 strikeouts. Those strikeouts are good because he's a pitcher. That's a big goal that he accomplished this weekend, and I admire him for it; not just that he did it, but that he was willing to say what he wanted to do out loud. The danger in saying something like that out loud is that you might not ever do it. Voicing your dream is a risky thing because you don't know how people might respond, and once you've put it out there, some people will be looking for you to fail. That's just the truth of the matter. However, if you aren't willing to say where you want to go, I'm not sure you're very likely to ever get there. If fear holds you captive, you're like our dog Junebug who stands at the top of the stairs, too afraid to walk down them to get to where her food bowl is.

Once again, we've been given a ribbon.

This time, the ribbon is green.

Why? It represents the green pasture to where the good shepherd leads his sheep.

Today, I invite you to write a word down on your green ribbon a place you want to go, a thing that you want to do, a state of well-being that you hope to achieve. Whatever or wherever it is, write it down, and as you write it down, imagine that you're in a place where you're safe, like a couch or a lap or in someone's arms where you can smell their smell and sense their presence and be reminded that fear is just a feeling that only holds us captive so long as we let it.

It happened to me four years ago that fear was cast out enough for me to dream by a smell.

Four years ago last weekend, I was in the final stages of accepting this position to come and be one of your pastors. In order for a pastor to do that, he or she must be examined by the Presbytery to make sure everyone understands what he or she is getting into. This Presbytery was worried that I didn't understand that the church I'd be serving in was a different place from the church I grew up in. They were worried I didn't know what I was getting into. Of course, they were right in a sense. A lot has changed over the last several years since I graduated high school as an active member of our youth group, but I told that Presbytery that this church still smells the same.

I'm not kidding.

There's a stairwell in this church that smells exactly the same way now that it did when I was a kid going down to Sunday school, and four years ago that smell reminded me that the Good Shepherd I was introduced to in this church when I was a child is still with me, and I don't need to be held captive by my troubles and my fears. I remembered that this week. I had to remember it again because it's been a very hard year and half for me and for us all, though I've realized again recently that my fears are only holding me back if I let them.

Sometimes I am so afraid that I forget who is with me, who is with us, and I fail to remember what's been promised, namely that "nothing can separate us from the love of God that is in Christ Jesus our Lord." Not famine. Not hardship. Not powers. Not height, nor depth, nor anything else in all creation. Not COVID, not politics, not division, not bad news. Nothing. Why? Because he is with us.

And we are in his presence now, so write a dream, a hope, a place you want to go, or a state of mind you hope to achieve. Write it down on your green ribbon and remember this: plenty of people had their doubts about us, but our church has just been voted the best place to worship in Cobb County for the third year in a row because he is still with us, and fear will not stop us from getting anywhere we are destined to go.

Where do you long to go?

Whom do you long to be?

Free from fear, write it down, and as the wind blows through our ribbons, our prayers will be lifted to Almighty God.

Amen.

Practice: Remember a place where you felt safe. What does that place look like? How does it smell? Who is there with you? Trusting that the Good Shepherd who smells like his sheep is with you right now, dare to allow yourself to dream. Where do you want to go? Whom do you want to be? Write it down on a ribbon or a piece of paper and release this prayer to God.

Prayer: *Almighty God, you were there with me from the very beginning, knitting me together in my mother's womb. You will be with me at the very end, welcoming me into the Kingdom of Heaven as a shepherd welcomes his sheep home to the sheepfold. Remind me again and again that you are always with me, walking beside me, and leading me beyond where I am to where I long to be. Amen.*

I AM The Resurrection and the Life
John 11: 17-27 and Ezekiel 37: 1-14

Preached on July 4, 2021 by Rev. Cassie Waits

Our God is endlessly creative. We need only peel back the first page of Scripture to see God cheerfully creating.

When we talk about God creating, we usually think of Genesis chapter 1:

> *"In the beginning, when God created the heavens and the earth, the earth was a formless void and darkness covered the face of the deep."* (NRSV)

This is only the beginning of the many creation accounts in our scripture! If you're a musician, like Larisa Dukes or Linda Bush, you might appreciate Psalm 8:

> *"O LORD our LORD, how majestic is your name in all the earth! When I consider your heavens, the work of your fingers… what is mankind that you are mindful of them?"* (NIV)

If you're a writer like Stacy Jensen or Bennett Frye, you might like John chapter 1:

> *"In the beginning was the word, and the word was with God, and the word was God."*

If you have an unquenchable thirst for knowledge, like Charlie Etheridge or Mrs. Florrie Corley, Proverbs 8 may be for you. Wisdom speaks and she says:

> *"The L*ORD *created me at the beginning of his work, Before the mountains and hills, the earth and the fields, the seas and the springs of water."* (NRSV, paraphrased for brevity)

If you like to build things, like Paul Phillips or Tim Hammond, you might prefer Job 38, where God appears to Job and reminds him:

> *I laid the foundation of the earth.*
> *I determined its measurements and stretched the line upon it.*
> *I sunk its bases and laid the cornerstone.* (NRSV, shifted to 1st person for clarity)

If you are grieving, you might draw comfort from Revelation 21:

> *"Then, I saw a new heaven and a new earth…and I heard a loud voice from the throne saying, 'See, the*

home of God is among mortals. He will wipe every tear from their eyes. Death will be no more...see, I am making all things new.'" (NRSV)

That's not all! We find yet another creation story in our Old Testament reading today: Ezekiel chapter 37.

Remember Ezekiel? He was a prophet in the 6th century B.C.: the timeframe when Babylon invades Jerusalem and conquers the surrounding land. Many people are captured and taken into exile. People like Daniel, Shadrach, Meshach, and Abednego. They wind up in Babylon – along with the prophet Ezekiel.

Ezekiel prophesies to people who have been uprooted in every way. They have left behind their homes, their land, their traditions, their temple. They are numb with grief, exhausted from fighting, and mourning those who died in the battle. They're going through the motions of life, but they're not really living.

In this moment, Ezekiel receives a vision of new creation.

Ezekiel is standing in a field full of bones. God commands him to speak, so he does. The bones rise up. Then, God commands him to speak again, so he does. A divine breath fills those dead bodies, and they come to life.

Ezekiel sees dead people…walking. *That's pretty creepy.*

This vision reminds me of a zombie movie. In America, we have lots of zombie movies.

We have:

Night of the Living Dead

Dawn of the Dead

Day of the Dead

House of the Dead

Land of the Dead

Army of the Dead

(There's a pattern!)

The entire *Resident Evil* series

Pet Sematary

Zombieland

And who can forget: *I Am Legend?*

A few years ago, zombie movies were all the rage.

If you ever wondered whether the Bible could be as exciting as an episode of *The Walking Dead*, now you know!

There's nothing more American than a good zombie movie, and there's certainly nothing more American than the Fourth of July.

Today is July 4th. Today, we celebrate our independence from Great Britain.

We're in good company. Over *60 countries* around the world celebrate their independence from Great Britain. Most of them, like Canada, Egypt, Afghanistan, and India, celebrate the day that the British Parliament signed a treaty or ratified an act to grant them independence. Most celebrate the day that power was officially handed over.

But not us.

We do not celebrate the day we *won* independence. (You may not even know what day that is!) Instead, we celebrate the day we *declared* independence, and with that declaration, we also declared war.

That's why, in July of 1776, our country was not celebrating its freedom with fireworks, we were trading fire with the British.

One of the most pivotal campaigns of the early Revolutionary War was the fight for control over New York City. General George Washington was adamant that the revolutionaries keep control of New York, but, in the fall of 1776, the British pushed 9,000 of Washington's soldiers out of Long Island and up the East River.

The revolutionaries regrouped in an area called Kip's Bay.

These were farmers and shopkeepers. They carried whatever weapons they could muster. As *Hamilton* playwright, Lin Manuel-Miranda, puts it, they were "outgunned, outmanned, outnumbered and outplanned." When the redcoats converged, this ragtag militia didn't just retreat, they *ran* away — to the mortification and disgust of General George Washington.

As Washington watched his army scatter in confusion and fear, he threw his hat to the ground and exclaimed, "Are these the men with which I am to defend America?"

Washington described the attack in a letter to John Hancock. Remember John Hancock? He signed the Declaration of Independence with the biggest signature so that King George would be sure to see it. That John Hancock. Washington wrote this:

> "If our troops would behave with tolerable bravery, the enemy would meet with a defeat ... but experience ... has convinced me that this is rather to be wished for than expected..." (From George Washington to John Hancock, September 16, 1776, https://founders.archives.gov)

Two months later, these fears came true. British forces took his last stronghold on Manhattan Island: a stronghold that was, regrettably, named Fort Washington.

By December 1776, support for the war had plummeted. The ranks of soldiers had shrunk to bare bones. There were rumors of mutiny, and our revolution was on the verge of collapse.

Washington did not have a vast army. He had a valley of dry bones.

It's hard to go on when you're stuck in the valley.

In our New Testament reading, Jesus visits the town of Bethany. Before he even gets there, Martha runs to meet him with news: her brother Lazarus – Jesus' friend – is dead.

She blames Jesus. "Lord, if you had been here my brother would not have died."

She's probably right. Jesus spends a lot of time healing the sick, and Martha knows what he has done and can do.

The answer Jesus gives is not terribly comforting. He says, "Your brother will rise up."

This isn't news. Martha already knows about end-time resurrection. Yes, her brother will rise – in the last days, in the far-off future.

Jesus is after something more immediate, though. He reminds Martha, "*I am* the resurrection and the life. Those who believe in me, even though they die, will live….and everyone who lives and believes in me will never die."

Martha, your brother will rise up, not in the far distant future, but *right now*. Your brother will rise up like the dry bones that Ezekiel saw. He will rise up because, in the presence of God, even dried up dead things spring to life.

On December 25, 1777, Christmas Day, George Washington led a contingent of his remaining soldiers in a daring and desperate journey across the icy Delaware river. He launched a surprise attack at Trenton, New York – and won. A few days later, he launched a second attack at Princeton – and won.

Those two victories filled America's lungs with hope and turned the tide of the war. The revolutionaries were cold, hungry, injured, exhausted, grieving, and scared.

Yet they rose up that day.

And we are called to rise as well.

This is not a command from a military general. It's an invitation from a loving, life-giving Savior.

Though our bodies are exhausted, Jesus calls us to rise up.

Though our joints ache, Jesus calls us to rise up.

Though our spirits are broken, we rise up.

Though our courage melts into fear, we rise up.

Though the enemy has us cornered, we rise up.

Though all hope seems lost, we rise up.

Even when we lie in the grave, we will rise up.

Because in the presence of Jesus, death and sin and decay fall away, and we are re-created anew.

Last summer, our church stepped up to serve as a weekly food bank distribution site. This outreach began with a small number of dedicated volunteers. One of the early volunteers was Fran Brailsford.

Fran didn't just show up because it was a nice mission; Fran showed up because she feels deeply and personally called to help the hungry. Fran took over as our greeter. In a couple of weeks, Fran has learned the names and stories of every person coming through our parking lot. If you ask Fran how she did it, she says: "Well, of course I know each person by name. These families are *my* family."

You might recognize Fran Brailsford's name. Our congregation has been praying for Fran for over a year because Fran is dying. Fran is dying of cancer, and she's made the decision not to treat it.

Week after week, Fran pushes through pain and exhaustion to show up for her families. She will tell you that on this difficult journey, the food bank ministry keeps her going. Fran's body may be growing weak, but her spirit is being made whole – over and over again.

Friends, this is resurrection. Yes, we believe that in the last days we will rise again, but we also believe that resurrection happens every single day. In the very face of death, our God plants seeds of *life*.

Speaking of dry bones, I am tired this morning. You might be, too.

I am tired because I was up at Montreat last week at a worship and music conference with several of our staff.

I carpooled up with our organist, Chohee. On the way home, I asked whether South Korea had an Independence Day, and this kicked off a conversation about the history of Korea. We made it all the way to 1950 and the Korean War. You may know that after the war, the country of Korea was divided, south from north, and a 2.5-mile swath of land was carved out as the Demilitarized Zone. This is a no man's land.

For almost 70 years, that land has been untouched by human beings. What you may not know, and what Chohee taught me, is that today that no-man's land, a place of death, is home to some 5,000 species of plants and animals. It has become a sanctuary.

Where we see a place of death, our God sees the makings of a garden.

When we accept Jesus as our Lord and Savior, we receive the gift of his love and freedom. We are no longer bound by sin and death. We are freed by the life-giving love of Christ.

Every day, at every step, we cling to that promise and claim the creative power of God.

Alleluia. Amen.

Practice: Consider your own valley of dry bones. Where do you need God to bring life to a situation or relationship? Write this valley on your ribbon and trust God to breathe new life into it.

Prayer: *Lord Jesus, forgive us for not trusting your power to make all things new. We offer you our places of death, that they might be transformed into places of life by your presence.*

Amen.

I AM the Way and the Truth and the Life
Exodus 13: 17-22 and John 14: 1-7

Preached on July 11, 2021 by Rev. Joe Evans

Do you hate to ask for directions?

Does your husband?

I hate to, so sometimes I just won't do it, even if I'm lost. Last week, I was in Montreat, North Carolina with several members of our staff for a Music and Worship Conference. For years, our church went there every winter for an annual retreat and sent the youth group to a conference there every summer. I've been there so many times that last week during the conference I was sure I knew where I was going. I was so sure that I couldn't ask for directions. It was a matter of pride. What's true about me is that sometimes I feel like I should know the way. That's pride or ego talking, but "I AM the way," he said to his disciples.

This is the fifth sermon in a series of eight focused on what some call the "I AM" statements of Jesus. Jesus describes himself in several different ways, and today we come to this significant statement, "I AM the way, and the truth, and the life." The Scripture lesson I just read where he describes himself this way comes from the Gospel of John.

I've read it many times.

At 90% of weddings, I've read 1st Corinthians 13, and at 90% of funerals, I've read this passage from the Gospel of John. Why? Maybe because it's only when we're faced with death that we're OK asking for directions. Only when confronted with that great journey into the unknown are we ready to confess that we don't already know the way, but, my friends, today let me say it clearly: whether it is from death to life, from lost to found, from uneducated to wise, on all great journeys we must be prepared to ask for directions.

Let Thomas be our example of how it's done.

Jesus says,

> *In my father's house there are many dwelling places. If it were not so, would I have told you that I go to prepare a place for you? And if I go and prepare a place for you, I will come again and will take you to myself, so that where I am there you may be also. And you know the way to the place where I am going.*

That phrase at the end makes an assumption: "And you know the way to the place where I am going, right?" It's like he's saying, "You've been paying attention, going to Sunday school, reading your Bible, singing your hymns, being a good girl or boy, and loving your neighbor, so you ought to know." Be careful here, for that phrase, "You ought to know," comes from a little voice inside all our heads and not from the lips of Jesus.

"You ought to know" is ego talking, and ego can't get us to the Promised Land.

It just sends us down a spiral of shame.

To get to the Promised Land, we must be ready to ask the Savior for directions, so think about what Thomas does here. He's the one willing to say, "Lord, we do not know the way."

That can be an embarrassing thing to say out loud.

Many people go through life very self-conscious about what they don't know or don't believe, so they don't broadcast it. I remember a story a friend told me. His son was getting married to a Roman Catholic woman. In order for the priest to do the wedding, he had to convert. That was fine with him. He was in love, so he was glad to, but he was getting lost in all these classes. He was hearing about all these saints and was getting confused. As he had been born Presbyterian, he wasn't used to any of it. Finally, he asked the priest who was teaching the class, "Just how much of this stuff do I actually have to believe?"

During the journey of faith, we all reach this point sooner or later.

The thing to remember when we reach this point is that the opposite of faith isn't doubt; the opposite of faith is certainty. Those are the words of Christian writer Ann Lamott. Do you know what she means by that? What she means is that there is a difference between knowing the way or thinking you know the way and following the One who is the way.

There is a difference, maybe a slight one, between knowing the Bible inside out and taking a step out into the unknown alongside the One who can walk on water.

There is a difference between thinking you have it all straight in your head and trusting the Savior with all your questions.

Thomas gets that.

In his unknowing, he shows us what being in a relationship with Jesus looks like.

With a certain kind of boldness – let's call it faith – he bravely asks the question that everyone else was too scared to ask: "Lord, we do not know where you are going. How can we know the way?"

Do you hear that?

Do you hear what he's asking?

Do you see what's faithful about asking a question like that?

This is how it's done.

Thomas has it right.

Do you know how I know he has it right? It's because Jesus doesn't push him away for his question. Jesus never shames Thomas for what he doesn't know. Instead, he just answers: "I AM the way," he said.

That's important for us to remember because in this world today, the social fabric is falling apart, and I believe it falls to the Church to show the world how to knit it back together; only right now, plenty of our brothers and sisters are all caught up in having the right answers, as though having the right answers were a substitute for being in right relationship. What I mean by that is that I'm back in school, and I'm having a hard time with some of what's required of me. I'm working towards my doctorate, and lately, all my classes have been on Zoom, which requires a certain level of computer literacy that I don't have. Not only that, but I also haven't been in class in a while, and a lot has changed since I was in seminary.

I joined this class, and I'd try to participate, but it seemed like I kept on putting my foot in my mouth. Without thinking, I offended a classmate. Not knowing what I had done, but just by reading her face, and seeing hurt there, I worried that I had slammed the door on a friendship before it even began. I contacted her, and I asked her, "Did I offend you? I didn't mean to. How can I make it right?"

This story might sound like the end of a friendship, but it wasn't.

In asking those questions, a friendship began because it doesn't matter whether you have all the right answers. Relationships can be built by having the courage to ask the right questions.

Have I offended you?

Why are you so upset?

Can you show me the way?

"I AM the way," he said. "I AM the way."

This statement reminds me of a certain kind of knowledge that's far more important than a grasp on facts or figures: a knowledge that sometimes we forget about. At the beginning of the pandemic, I was honored to talk with Meri Kate Marcum. Meri Kate is an elder on the session, so she's one of our church's elected leaders. She's also a seminary student, so she's training to be a pastor, and she's the director of the preschool over at the Methodist Church. At the beginning of the pandemic, she called me, and we were talking about preschools: who was doing what and what should be done. Meri Kate had already been talking with Betsy Sherwood, our preschool director, and the two of them were on the same page. They were both feeling like there wasn't much of a point to having virtual preschool, even though it was technically possible to do it, just as the elementary, middle, high schools, and colleges had.

Unlike those schools, "virtual preschool doesn't make any sense," they said, "because the main thing you need to learn in preschool is how to get along with your classmates, and you can't do that virtually." Now, you can learn some important things virtually, but:

You can't learn how to share.

You can't learn to keep your hands to yourself.

You can't learn to apologize.

You can't learn how to make friends.

"I AM the way," he said. What does he mean? He means don't worry so much about what you know or don't know. Worry more about asking the right questions that build up the right relationships because we're all heading towards the father's house with many rooms, and if we can't learn how to live together now, sharing that great big house is going to get difficult.

Have you ever lived in a house with a know-it-all?

One of my favorite proverbs from Scripture is Proverbs 21: 9:

> *It is better to live on the roof of a house than in it with a contentious wife.*

Had a woman written that proverb, it might have said, "It's better to live locked in the bathroom than with a man who thinks he's never wrong."

How dangerous it is to go through life with certainty.

How foolish it is to rush to conclusions.

Have you ever thought about how much damage false assumptions do to the world around us? Yet, people walk around thinking that they've got it all figured out already, certain that they know the way while the road to a better future is paved by those who are willing to ask the Savior the right question: "Lord, we don't know where you are going. How can we know the way?"

Clearly, we don't.

We don't know the way to equality, and what we think we know about people who look different than we do is keeping us from getting there.

We don't know the way to peace, and what we think we know about our enemies is keeping us from getting there.

We don't know the way to heaven, and what we think we know about heaven and who is going there is keeping us from it.

Let us be bold, then, to ask the Savior for directions.

Today you've been given another ribbon. This one is supposed to be orange. You might be looking at the color ribbon you received thinking, "Whoever called this ribbon orange doesn't know his colors. Maybe he should go back to preschool." Gold looked like orange when I picked it out. I'm sorry. What I want you to do with your whatever colored ribbon is this: write down a question you'd like to ask Jesus.

Did you know that you can do that?

Of course you can because your questions, your needs, your secrets, your shames, your fears, they won't keep you from having a relationship with our God. Voicing them to him is the way to start one.

"I AM the way, and the truth, and the life," which means you don't have to be.

You don't have to have it all together to be worthy of his love.

You don't have to know it all to be precious in his sight.

Take security in his boundless love and ask. Write your question, and find that in trusting Him with it, you'll receive from the Lord far more than an answer.

Amen.

Practice: By yourself and without the shame of wondering what anyone thinks, allow yourself to write down your big questions. They might be things like, "Am I a good mother?" "Am I going to heaven?" "Have I done enough?" "Why did you take him from me?" Whatever your questions are, get them out from the dark recess of your mind and put them on a ribbon or a piece of paper. Trust God with your questions and know that a good question is the beginning of a good relationship.

Prayer: *Almighty God, I am sometimes afraid to ask for directions. I am sometimes ashamed of what I don't know. Remind me that knowing always begins with asking, and that having asked the deep questions, you will walk beside me from this place of doubt and fear all the way to the Father's House where you have prepared my room. Amen.*

I AM the Vine
Isaiah 5: 1-7 and John 15: 1-8

Preached on July 18, 2021 by Rev. Joe Evans

Have you ever heard of Cecil Collins? I learned about him last Tuesday from a *Marietta Daily Journal* article about Evander Holyfield. Evander Holyfield, world heavyweight champion boxer and Atlanta resident, mentioned him when talking with Cobb Chamber of Commerce Chair John Loud last Monday.

Apparently, Cecil Collins is a white boy who Evander Holyfield just couldn't beat.

Holyfield was ten or eleven the first time Cecil Collins beat him, and after the fight he went home crying, ready to never box again.

He said, "My mamma let me cry for about two minutes. After that, she asked, 'What happened?'"

"I lost, and I quit," he answered.

Every kid goes through something like this, so all parents have been through this with their kids. Maybe what the kids don't know is that at least some of the time we'd like to let you quit so we don't have to drive you to practice anymore, but we can't let you do that, so Mrs. Holyfield made him go back to boxing. However, then Collins beat him again.

This time, it was his coach who talked him out of quitting. I guess Holyfield now knew better than to go straight to his mom, so he went to his coach instead.

His coach said, "[Why are you quitting? You haven't lost.] You lose when you stop. [You lose when] you don't do it [any] more. Setback paves the way for comeback."

That's good advice.

Obviously, Holyfield listened, and what I want to point out, thinking of Cecil Collins, is that Holyfield grew up to beat not just Cecil Collins but 44 out of the 57 he faced as a professional boxer. He is today the only professional fighter to win the heavyweight championship four times, surpassing the record set by Muhammad Ali, making him one of the greatest boxers of all time, and yet he also got pruned.

Expect to be pruned.

That's one important point that this passage from the Gospel of John makes. Expect to be pruned, and don't mistake being pruned from being cut from the vine.

"I AM the vine," he said.

This is the seventh sermon in a series of eight focusing on what Bible scholars call the "I AM" statements of Jesus. This is the seventh statement that Jesus uses to describe himself: "I AM the vine," he said, "and you are the branches." Even the branches that bear fruit must be pruned so that they can bear more fruit, and how important it becomes that we are able to tell the difference between being pruned and being cut off from the vine.

Do you know anyone who has trouble telling the difference?

If you know me then you know someone.

How many times have I hit a bump in the road professionally and been ready to quit?

How many times have I made a mistake and been too embarrassed to apologize, so I wanted to just quit on a person?

How many times have I suffered and wondered if God had quit on me?

We parents all make fun of our kids who sometimes act like it's the end of the world when they're disappointed. She doesn't make the team, and she acts like her life is over. Someone breaks his heart, and he can't leave his bedroom. They act like this because that's how it feels, and it feels that way to their parents, too, but enough bad things have happened to their parents for them to realize that bad things are normal.

All the time, bad things are happening to us.

Day after day, we must let go and move on.

It's not all tragic, for every branch that bears fruit must be pruned to bear even more, and just because some parts of us are dying, that doesn't mean we are dying.

That doesn't mean we have to quit.

That doesn't mean it's all over.

A book I love is *Zen and the Art of Motorcycle Maintenance*. It was rejected by publishers 121 times and has since sold 5 million copies worldwide. This is just one of many books that was famously rejected to go on to huge success. Author of *Harry Potter*, J. K. Rowling, who has sold 450 million books, was rejected by her first 12 publishers. Stephen King threw his first book in the garbage, rejecting it himself. It was then rejected 30 times before being picked up by Doubleday Publishing and selling over 1 million copies.

Then there's Michael Jordan.

Some say he's the greatest basketball player who ever lived, but did you know that Michael Jordan didn't make the high school varsity basketball team the first time he tried out?

Now he says, "[That's when it all started.] It all started when coach Pop Herring cut me [from the team]."

After not making the team, Jordan went home to cry, but years later, then a superstar on Jay Leno in 1997, he said, "Everybody goes through disappointments; it's how you overcome those disappointments. I just wasn't good enough. [Today I know that was] the best thing that could have happened to me: to get cut because [getting cut] made me go back and get caught up with my skill level."

Now, I'm not the Michael Jordan of preaching, but I assure you, I've gotten better too, and so much of my improvement is a result of my failure.

I was in a club for aspiring preachers in college, and the club sponsor took me to the local retirement home to preach one Sunday morning. On the way back to campus, the only good thing he could think to say was, "You preached for 17 minutes. That was about the right amount of time."

I've been doing it like that ever since.

Did you know that it's OK to fail?

That it's good to be pruned?

That you weren't born perfect and so you must get better every day and every hour?

Some of us go through life so afraid of criticism that we let it break us. Others of us go through life so hungry for praise that we avoid ever taking a risk.

The parable makes this much plain: getting pruned is a part of life.

Getting pruned helps us bear more fruit.

Getting pruned doesn't mean we're cut off from the vine.

"I AM the vine," he said, and do you know what else he said? "I will never leave you nor forsake you." "I will be with you, even until the end of the age," and according to the Apostle Paul: "Nothing will separate you from the love of God that is in Christ Jesus our Lord."

Now, that doesn't mean you're perfect.

That doesn't mean you don't have more to learn.

That doesn't mean you don't have anything to apologize for. You do. I do, but we can apologize because doing something bad doesn't mean we're bad. Making a mistake doesn't mean I'm a mistake. Failing a test doesn't make me a failure. A rejection doesn't disqualify me. It certainly doesn't disqualify me from being loved.

Who reminds you of that?

Good parents remind kids of that all the time. Evander Holyfield's mom wouldn't let him quit. He got beat twice by Cecil Collins. After their third fight, when Holyfield won, his mama gave him permission to quit boxing if he wanted to, but he kept going. Who has helped you keep going?

Today, you have a purple ribbon. Grapes are purple, and we're blessed with people who help us produce more of them. When we are pruned, we produce more. When we remember that we're connected to the vine, we produce more. Who has helped you remember that you're still connected to the vine?

I'd like for you to write their names on your purple ribbon because it's a miraculous thing they've done for us, isn't it?

Of course, there's a time to quit. Some people in my life have helped me quit certain things. I was never going to be a heavyweight boxing champion. I was never going to make the Atlanta Braves, but I once tried to quit basketball in the middle of a game. I was ten or eleven, and I couldn't make a shot. My dad pulled me over to the side and said, "Did you know that the best players in the NBA miss half their shots?" That's true.

Did you know that while Babe Ruth hit 714 home runs, he struck out over 13,000 times?

Did you know that the first time Abraham Lincoln ran for political office he came in 8th?

I've wanted to quit being a preacher a time or two, and I'm very thankful to those people who wouldn't let me. I told you already that I once preached a sermon where the only good thing about it was that it was brief. "If you can't be good, be brief," my preaching professor once said. I also once preached a good sermon, and a mentor of mine said, "That sermon made God smile." That compliment makes me tear up just thinking of it, and had I quit, I never would have heard it. Had I not been pruned, I never would have heard it either.

"I AM the vine," he said, and being pruned once or twice does not cut us off from him.

Who has reminded you of that?

The whole nation of Israel was reminded of that by the Psalms and the Prophets. We read about it from our first Scripture lesson: a vine who yielded wild grapes. This vine represents a people who failed. They failed to measure up, they turned away from whom they were created to be. God expected justice from them but saw bloodshed instead. God expected righteousness, but instead heard the cry of the innocent suffering at the hands of the powerful. What the prophet is saying here is that the people deserved to be cut off.

Not just pruned, but torn down, pulled up, and tilled under.

What vineyard owner preserves a vine who produces wild grapes?

Who sows bloodshed and abuses the weak?

Yet our faith is not about what we deserve.

Our faith is about a grace greater than all our sin.

Who has reminded you of that?

Who has remined you that by being pruned, you might still bear good fruit?

That through hardship, we might find a better way to be?

That while he has reason to, Christ has not given up on his people yet, and by his grace, we are invited to try and try and try again?

Who has helped you remember that his love for you is as resilient as that vine in the yard that just won't die and keeps coming back?

Write their names down on your purple ribbon and give thanks to God for them.

Amen.

Practice: When have you been pruned, disappointed, discouraged, or depressed? Who was there to lift you back up? What did he/she say? Or was it just his/her presence? Isn't just a person's presence a gift from God? Think of that person, write his/her name down on a ribbon or a piece of paper, and give thanks to God for him/her. Then, pledge to be that person to someone else.

Prayer: Almighty God, we give you thanks for those who walk beside us, reminding us that you are never far in times of trouble. Keep us aware of your presence in our lives, especially in the midst of suffering and hardship. Amen.

I AM
Exodus 3: 1-14 and John 18: 1-11

Preached on July 25, 2021 by Rev. Joe Evans

Most days when it's nice out, and even sometimes when it's not as nice, I ride my bike here to the church. When I get here, I park it in the bike rack right outside that Mike Clotfelter installed about four years ago now.

Just having the option of riding a bike to work is a benefit of living close by that I'm grateful for, and this blessing only comes with a couple challenges:

1. How will I get home if it's raining?

2. How do I survive riding over the Harris Hines Bridge?

One Monday morning, I was riding here. I got to that bridge. You know the one I'm talking about. It's the bridge right behind the church that takes Kennesaw Avenue over the 120 Loop. Going over that bridge is the part of the ride that scares me the most because the road narrows, and people speed up to get over the railroad tracks, so I almost always illegally ride on the sidewalk. Well, that Monday, there were two people walking on the sidewalk already. I first came up behind Ginny Brogan, a member here, who tolerated me as I squeezed past her on the narrow sidewalk. Up ahead was the other, a man I didn't know. As I passed by him on my bike, he said, just loud enough for me to hear, "You know it's illegal to ride a bike on the sidewalk."

I didn't know this man, and his words struck me, so I thought about stopping to apologize or explain myself, only then the thought occurred to me, "What if he asks who I am and where I'm going?"

How is it going to look to this man I've never met before? How is it going to reflect on this church if I so blatantly disregard the standards of public safety on my way here?

What if he said, "Well, I was thinking of going to visit First Presbyterian Church, but now that the preacher nearly pushed me off the sidewalk and into oncoming traffic, I think I'd rather not?" For that reason, I just kept riding, but I still think about it.

I still think about almost running this man off the sidewalk with my bicycle because, while maybe it's not as bad as cutting off someone's ear, still, it is another instance where I must wonder how well the Gospel is being preached through the actions of those who call themselves Christians.

Think about the slave Malchus.

The Bible takes the time to give us his name, which is a sign of how important he is to remember.

We just read: "Simon Peter, who had a sword, drew it, struck the high priest's slave, and cut off his right ear. The slave's name was Malchus," and he was doing nothing more than minding his own business, obeying his master's wishes, so what did he think about the Prince of Peace when his right-hand man, Simon Peter, comes at him with a sword?

How was the Gospel proclaimed in that moment?

How was the Kingdom advanced?

On whom has Christ built his church?

Do you know that line?

The first time Peter fully recognized Jesus for who he was, he said, "You are the Messiah, the Son of the living God." Excited, Jesus then said to him, "You are Peter, and on this rock, I will build my church, and the gates of Hades will not prevail against it." When Jesus makes this declaration to Peter, it's a Spirit-filled moment recorded in Scripture, and there's even more to it if you can read Greek, the language the account was originally written in. In Greek, the word for rock is *Petros* or 'Peter.' The name 'Peter' just means 'rock,' which is why Jesus names the man formally known as Simon 'Peter.'

His name says it all: "He is the rock" Christ's Church is built upon, but the rock cut off a man's ear. What do you make of that?

Another important play on words that I believe helps explain an important point is an easy one to miss in our second Scripture lesson because this one hinges on our ability to read Hebrew. When "a detachment of soldiers together with police from the chief priest and the Pharisees [were led by Judas] with lanterns and torches and weapons," Jesus asked, "Whom are you looking for?"

They said, "Jesus of Nazareth," and Jesus said, "I AM."

That's not what we read in English because a literal translation of the ancient language doesn't make much sense, so just a moment ago, we read Jesus' response as, "I am he." That's not an exact translation. What I want you to know is that in our first Scripture lesson, when Moses asks God, "Whom shall I say sent me?" God says, "Tell them I AM sent you." In our second Scripture lesson, Jesus is quoting God because that's who he is.

As he's being arrested, he's letting them know that he is the God of Abraham and Sarah, Miriam and Moses, Shadrach, Meshach, and Abednego.

He's the power behind the burning bush and the pillar of flames that led the people through the wilderness.

Incarnate in human flesh, he is the first and the last, the beginning and the end, the one who created this world, who still sustains it, and who works through human history to redeem it again and again and again.

Bible scholars will tell you that here Jesus invokes the divine name, which explains why the intimidating band of armed men who had come to arrest him "stepped back and fell to the ground" before a collection of threadbare disciples led by the Prince of Peace. These soldiers and police officers kneel before him because they know that they are not God, but he just said he is. "I AM," he said.

Now I go back to Peter, who is the rock that Christ's church is built upon.

Did he really cut off a man's ear?

Yes, he did.

Can you really build a church on Peter?

Of course you can, so long as Peter and everyone else remembers that Peter's not God. "I AM," says Jesus. "I AM."

This is the final Sunday of an eight-week sermon series focused on the "I AM," statements of Jesus. Week after week, we've focused on these phrases that Jesus uses to describe himself. This summer, we've thought about how Jesus says, "I AM the bread of life. I AM the light of the world. I AM the gate, the good shepherd, the resurrection and the life, the way and the truth and the life," and last Sunday, "I AM the vine." Now we reach the 8th and final statement, which is just plain, "I AM."

To think about this one is a little bit harder.

You have to reach a little bit further to understand what he means. Even scholars typically only deal with the first seven of these statements, but Rev. Cassie Waits, who came up with this series and the idea for the ribbons, added this 8th one because saying, "I AM" also goes so far in Jesus' effort to describe himself to us. Moreover, this description goes a long way in helping us understand who we are. With this statement, Jesus is explicitly saying, "I am the same God who spoke to Moses out of the burning bush and led the Hebrew people out of slavery," though what I want to focus on this Sunday is what's implicit in this statement because it's also as though Jesus is saying, "I am God, and you are not."

Do you know anyone who gets confused about that?

Some people do.

I have a message for those members of a neighboring church who find themselves in the news week after week. I'm not telling you anything you don't already know when I say that Mount Bethel United Methodist Church is in the headlines. Some are disappointed in the pastor who is refusing to do what the bishop says. Others are disappointed in the bishop for making this move for reasons of church politics rather than for the well-being of the congregation. Both factions make a fair point, only here's what's most important for any frustrated church members to remember: neither the bishop nor the pastor is God.

"I AM," Jesus said.

We must remember that.

If we don't, we'll stand to be disappointed again and again, for no human being can stand up to divine standards.

We're not perfect. "I AM," Jesus said.

We're not always selfless, but "I AM" Jesus says.

We're not free from ambition, ego, narcissism, pride, or human error, though Jesus says, "I AM." Plus, to quote the pastor who did our premarital counseling, "If you go looking for flaws in your partner you're going to find them," and that goes for your pastor, your doctor, your kids, yourself, your politicians, the CDC, the World Health Organization, CNN, the School Board, the Rotary Club, or anything else run by human beings. Some might ask, "Then whom should we be listening to? Is it just eeny, meeny, miny, mo?"

No. It's "and he is it."

We aren't perfect, but "I AM," he said.

"I AM."

What do with that? I'll tell you.

Don't confuse preachers and Jesus.

Don't confuse politicians and the Savior.

Don't confuse doctors and God.

Don't think that you're more powerful than you are.

You just aren't that powerful, and neither is anybody else. Amazing things happen through you. That's true. Still, we try too hard. We hold too tightly. We can't let go. We deny our shortcomings.

This week you were given a blue ribbon. Blue is for the color of Mary, the mother of Jesus. I think about her and all she knew about her baby; how she knew that she wasn't the one to put the world right.

No, she wasn't.

"I AM," Jesus said.

That's what I want you to write about this Sunday on your ribbon. What do you need his help with?

There's that country song, "Jesus, Take the Wheel." That's not very good advice when it comes to driving a car, but there are so many moments where that's the best advice in the world. Why? Because sometimes, with us, it's impossible, while nothing will be impossible with the one who said, "I AM."

When you get down to it, who is he to you?

Or who do you long that he would be?

What is the thing you know you can't do and long that he would help you with?

What is the shortcoming that you have that you need his grace to fill?

There have been a million pages written to get down to this one essential theological reality that any child here could sing:

We are weak, but he is strong.

Give to the Lord your weakness.

Being a Christian isn't about perfection. If you want to be a Christian in your heart, then kneel before him. Surrender. There comes a moment when we must stop thinking, "If I could just be the right person; if I could just get the right answer; if I would just try harder or be better." Christ has built his Church on the rock of imperfect Peter, on the reality of our weakness, for our weakness points to his strength.

Where are you weak?

How can he help you?

Moses said, "You can't send me. I can't speak," yet what did God do through him?

Write down your weakness on your ribbon, and just as Christ gave Malchus back his ear, so may his grace heal the wounds inflicted on the world by imperfect people just like us.

Give to him your weakness. Write it down on your ribbon, and may it become a foundation for his strength at work in your life.

Amen.

Practice: Don't be afraid of your weakness. Don't try to hide it. Think about where you are weak, where you need help, what you are struggling with, and write it down on a ribbon or a piece of paper. Acknowledge that you can't fix everything, for the words of the Serenity Prayer are good and true: we need the wisdom to know the difference between what we can change and what we cannot. Hand to God what you cannot change and entrust it to his power.

Prayer: *God, grant me the serenity to accept the things I cannot change, the courage to change the things I can, and the wisdom to know the difference. Amen.*

Final Thoughts

The title of this series, "I AM," draws its roots both from the Gospel of John and from the divine name given to Moses in Exodus 3. At the burning bush, Moses hears the holy name of God: YHWH. Most English Bibles render this phrase, "I am who I am."

Our Theologian-in-Residence, Dr. Brennan Breed, notes that a more precise rendering of YHWH is, "I will be who I will be." In the original Hebrew text, God's name carries a sense of future possibility. Far from a static, unchanging force, God is active and alive, moving through and responding to our world.

Together, we have studied eight expressions of God's presence, and we have been reminded that our God cannot be reduced to a single image or a single attribute. Consider this a starting point – an invitation – for continued reflection on the many ways God is present among us. How is God showing up in your life? How is God showing up in the world?

God will be who God will be. Thanks be to God. Amen.

www.ingramcontent.com/pod-product-compliance
Lightning Source LLC
Chambersburg PA
CBHW071505070526
44578CB00001B/443